PRE MARITAL SEX

AVE MARIA PRESS • NOTRE DAME, INDIANA 46556

Nihil Obstat: John L. Reedy, C.S.C.
Censor Deputatus

Imprimatur: Most Rev. Leo A. Pursley, D.D.
Bishop of Fort Wayne-South Bend

Library of Congress Catalog Card No: 72-76479

International Standard Book No: 0-87793-045-7

© 1972 Ave Maria Press. All rights reserved

Photography: Page 3, *Vern Sigl;* 8, 50, *Robert Strobridge;* 18, 70, *Paul Schrock;* 32, *Connors;* 62, *Anthony Rowland;* 80, *Bryan Moss.*

Printed in the United States of America

CONTENTS

Preface 7

1. Let's Talk About It 9
2. The Meaning of the Sex Act 19
3. Is "Love" All That Matters? 33
4. Why Wait Till Marriage? 51
5. What Does God Want? 63
6. A Direction to Follow 71
7. I Love You Forever! 81

FATHER EDWIN G. DASCHBACH draws on five years' experience teaching Marriage and Family courses to juniors and seniors at Cathedral Co-educational High School in Trenton, N.J., and to CCD students from the nearby public high schools. He also teaches at the Divine Word Seminary in Bordentown, New Jersey.

Father Daschbach received his college and seminary training at the Divine Word Seminaries in Conesus, N.Y., and Techny, Illinois, and has attended Loyola and DePaul Universities in Chicago. In addition to philosophy and theology degrees, he holds a master's degree from the Fordham Institute of Religious Education.

PREFACE

Much has already been written about premarital sex, and so the author has no intention of having his contribution substitute for other standard works on the subject. He presents his reflections rather as an appendage—something added to more detailed and complete presentations.

One of his main hopes is that the ideas presented here will be given a good deal of thought. The book is not meant to be read swiftly, but to be pondered and discussed. If these thoughts are able to help the same type of students whose questions and problems inspired the endeavor, the author will consider the venture successful.

Mr. Ernest Collyer deserves special mention for his grammatical corrections and sentence revision. He appeared at times to be a complete co-author! Helen Miarowski also deserves special mention: her time was given cheerfully in an already busy schedule.

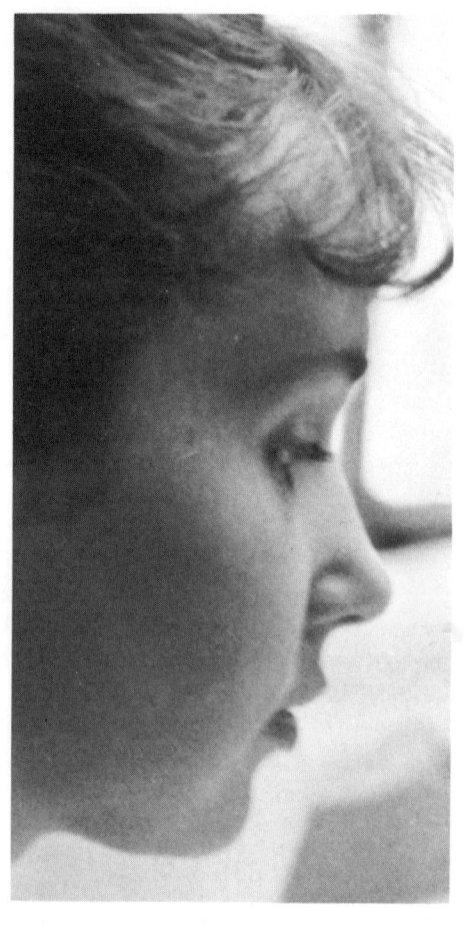

1 LET'S TALK ABOUT IT

"When I was a boy of 14, my father was so ignorant I could hardly stand to have the old man around. But when I got to be 21, I was astonished at how much he had learned in 7 years."
—Mark Twain

FOR the past few years I have had the opportunity to discuss the topic of premarital sex with some 800 high school seniors. Most classes were not so small as I would have liked, therefore I was unable to hear the reactions of all the students. But I found many who were quite open and without a doubt honest and sincere. These students helped me to understand some of the problems and questions that others besides themselves were considering.

An idea that I heard expressed several times left me with some uneasiness while writing these pages. That idea was the fear of "indoctrination." Some students had somehow developed a definite hesitancy about acquiring views on the question of sex before marriage because, as they put it, they would be unable as a result to think for themselves. They seemed to be asking for a blank page in this regard so that they would be able to make up their own minds freely.

We could take time to search out and make guesses—perhaps quite accurate—on the cause of such an objection. It would not take much research, however, to discover

Let's Talk About It

that a major problem is probably with us adults. We who have taught students in classes, or dealt with them more closely as parents, may have turned youth off by our doctrinaire "We adults have spoken. That's it!" approach. We have acted as our parents (or grandparents) did when stuffing a goose for the holiday dinner. Like that goose, our youth have not been given an active part to play. We have not respected them. We have not allowed them to voice their objections or offer valid insights. We have not allowed them to learn in the way in which they seek to learn—through discussion in a thoughtful manner.

Thus, some young people for whom these pages are intended may not bother to read them. But together with those who have suffered with me so far, I would like to consider that objection of "indoctrination."

The fear persists that being taught specific rules and directives will keep young people from really thinking for themselves. Guilt feelings are associated with certain kinds of behavior because of such information they received in the past. The idea is to be able to approach situations without such preconditioned "hang-ups," and to try to express love in a way that nobody will get hurt . . . "in the way I honestly feel will be the best for myself and for the other person."

I am afraid this search is utopian and bound to end in frustration on, at least, two counts. First, as social individuals within a society, we cannot help but imbibe consciously or unconsciously values of that culture. Environment conditions us more deeply than on the mere conscious level. If I were to direct all my powers at controlling that conscious level so as to prevent my learning specific directives, I would still miss the unconscious learning level. I could, of course, take flight from society and live a hermit's existence and, providing I do so early enough in life, I could possibly avoid much of the preconditioning that I feel limits the free direction of my life. Such a scheme would seem to have value in eliminating some of the evils that arise from social conditions. But what about the good things we can learn from social conditioning? Are there not many things I have learned from the experience of others that have helped me grow as a person—have helped me to know and love myself as well as others?

Second, I wonder how reasonable it is to expect to have a good understanding of what it means to love without seriously considering the "wisdom of the past." We do not carry over our objection against past

Let's Talk About It

wisdom into other spheres of life. What scientist will be able to continue the search for cures and progress for mankind if he refuses to accept what his predecessors and contemporary colleagues have discovered? He accepts their discoveries and tries to build on them.

The objection here might be that such discoveries are proved scientifically. Anyone can readily see how "they work." But, really, is there that much difference in the area of values? Can we honestly believe that the directions we are given by our elders (and many peers) are *unproved?* If they were, why would they be urging us to follow them? The accusation that people are trying to deny the young the joys they never had, or to uphold old values just because they are old or nostalgic, simply does not stand up. It would be much closer to the truth to try to realize that adults are honestly and sincerely trying to do exactly what youth tries to do when someone is seen to be in "need." They are trying to help.

Man needs direction in his life. This follows naturally from his unique type of existence. Unlike other forms of animals, man often does not know by instinct how to apply his drives properly or even practically. He has to be taught. Other animals know automatically, for example, how and when to express their sexual drives. When the female is "in heat," the male is sexually stirred, and only then mating occurs. There is no real "love" in such animals. The reason is, quite simply, that love is a characteristic of a being that can choose freely. Hence, his drive for union with the other sex of his species cannot be simply biological . . . not if he is to be true to his whole nature. His physical side will *spontaneously* find itself drawn to its partner counterpart, but his volitional and cognitive side has to be *trained* in order to function properly. It is this latter aspect of man that makes his sexual union so utterly different from the union of other animals. It makes literally "all the difference in the world." Sexual intercourse, for him, is raised from a purely biological function to heights of dignity with deep significance.

We can see here the need for education. Personal experience cannot adequately teach this level of self. The process would be too long and riddled with pitfalls. Too much is at stake to risk such dangers. Man's life is limited, and "you only go around once." Hence, the desire to "live with gusto" requires direction if that "gusto" is to be worthy of man's true dignity.

We should try to remember that despite the vast differences in our contemporary

Let's Talk About It

culture, with our scientific discoveries and achievements, the human being living through such changes is basically the same as always. His nature is still "human" with all that term signifies. If his knowledge is genuine, it must necessarily lead not to pride and complete self-sufficiency, but to a deeper awareness of his human needs. The more he learns, the more he realizes he has yet to learn. Knowledge and advancement in one area—for example, science—are not always paralleled in other areas. We can have a genius in microbiology or nuclear physics who is nevertheless emotionally immature. Both areas—the intellectual and emotional—contribute to the mature adult. We need direction in both.

The budding scientist requires years of intensive training. If he tries to skip it and rely merely on his own personal laboratory efforts, he will hardly develop properly in his field. The emotional area of his life requires similar direction if he is to be adequately "adjusted." A wealth of information and guidance is available here for all who open themselves to it. The intent of this book is to try to offer some—with the hope that thoughtful reflection and discussions will allow the ideas not only to become meaningful directives in themselves, but also to give rise to other concepts that will prove effective in promoting proper sexual development.

Experience and reflection have been concentrating on "love" for a long time. People living today are not the first to direct their attention to it. And individuals sharing past experiences and doing all the *laborious* reflection have come upon some ideas that can be extremely beneficial for those who take the time to listen. The newness of today's situations should not blind us to their ingrained similarity to situations of yesterday. In a later chapter we will consider some of the "wisdom" that has resulted from past thinking and experience and try to see how it gives some insight into the question of premarital sex.

For Youth Only

We feel the adolescent years are very important for your future adult life. As you grow, as you "become" more of a person in your journey through life, you will experience many things. It cannot be emphasized too strongly how important it is to regulate those experiences responsibly and thoughtfully. All that you do affects what you become. Experiences are not realities in a vacuum. They are part and

Let's Talk About It

parcel of one's life and intimately affect that life—for good or bad. They determine what kind of adults young people will become. Handle those everyday experiences carefully, and your happy and well-adjusted adulthood will forever be in debt to your youth.

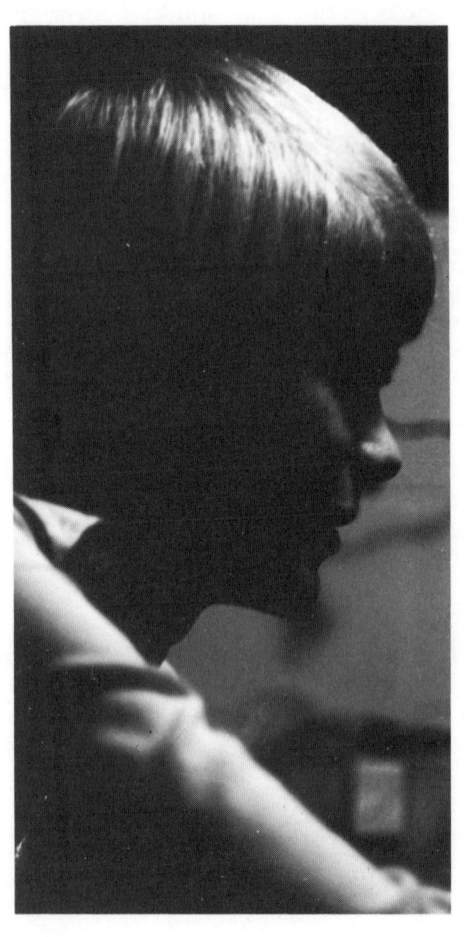

THE MEANING OF THE SEX ACT 2

THE physical act of sexual intercourse is a quite uncomplicated reality. If we look at it only casually and superficially, it can become—though in itself capable of one of the profoundest and most meaningful colloquies available to man—nothing more than a momentary "high," a self-centered "using" of another person for the sake of one's own self-gratification.

But what is wrong with such self-gratification? Unfortunately, this question is in itself symptomatic of the problem: Too many people can see only the *image,* its "seemingness"; they miss the reality. The true meaning is usually shielded, quite delicately, from the superficial and is capable of being penetrated only by those who make the required effort.

And effort is *all* that it takes. There are realities in life whose secrets are closed to all but the most gifted, but the majority of our everyday experiences yield their truths to the rest of us if we just take the time to do the necessary searching. The hectic rat race of contemporary American society actually demands that man make this effort. If he is to remain the meaningful controller of his own destiny, he must learn to separate himself from this environment in thoughtful silence and reflection. The beauties of life and of our everyday

The Meaning of the Sex Act

experiences are too precious for us to dismiss as if we were automatons. That is the precise danger and unfortunate reality for many.

There is beautiful meaning inherent in the very act of sexual intercourse. That meaning is *always* present. It is something built in, which speaks itself without the words and actions that each partner brings to the relationship.

I can ruin that self-spoken significance of the action itself with my selfish attitude. I can cause the act to degenerate from a beautiful symbol and manifestation of love and total dedication to a meaningless or selfish gesture.

It is necessary to try to discover exactly what *is* the actual core meaning expressed by the very act of sexual intercourse.

When persons perform the sexual action, they are expressing in the fullest measure a total gift of self. This is not the same as the gift spoken of by Christ in his farewell love-feast: "A man can have no greater love than to lay down his life for his friends" (Jn 15:13). That is indeed full self-giving. It does not always occur in an instant of swift self-immolation, but can extend over a long period of day-to-day living. The people who sacrifice themselves nobly in this manner are called "saints."

But the total gift of self inherent in the sexual act is on a different plane. In performing the action the man states: "Accept me, I am yours. I can give nothing further, physically, than this gift of my body and the expression of my manhood that it contains. Our union is bodily complete." Since man is not pure body, however, but exists as a conscious self with mind and intellect, he cannot separate *himself* from such an act. The whole person, not just his body, is involved. Passion may influence the conscious directing of the act, but it is, nevertheless, himself that is given. This is what the act explicitly says.

The mind, the controlling force of the self, can withhold itself. It can subtract from the basic meaning so that my act does not actually mean what it actually says. In such cases, I am then acting out a lie! I am using a beautiful expression of truth, honesty, and complete dedication in a dishonest way. I am bringing falsehood into truth, "seemingness" into open honesty, and incompleteness into total dedication. In an age of increasing artificiality I am adding my own depreciation in the area of human value. I am undermining an expression of what ought to be completely genuine. I am beginning to destroy a reality whose value may never be the same for me again.

The Meaning of the Sex Act

I cannot play with the sacred—and intercourse is sacred whether from a spiritual or simply human viewpoint—and walk away unaffected. When I treat the sacred casually and depart from it with the same casualness, I deprive myself of an experience of beauty not only here and now but in the future as well.

We experiment with everything today. Our advanced technology is a marvelous witness to that fact. But we fail to realize that not *everything* can be the object of experimentation without a resultant loss in another sphere—even perhaps in the same sphere at a later moment. Certain experiences we have today may actually prevent a much nobler experience tomorrow. This must always be kept in mind when dealing with human values.

Sexual intercourse is a perfect example of this truth: Its deep significance can readily be dulled, tarnished, even possibly lost if it is engaged in by individuals not properly prepared psychologically or emotionally, by individuals using it perhaps casually and superficially. Is this not the case of the individual who has run the playboy circuit and then, against all the playboy's directives, falls genuinely in love —only to discover that he cannot relate sexually with this woman he loves, at last, so honestly? He cannot be fulfilled in the sexual act. He cannot reach a satisfactory climax unless he imagines himself in one of his former liaisons. The sexual expression has been robbed of its beautiful significance, and he cannot, therefore, associate it with this woman who is "so different, so far above all the rest."

* * *

Does the individual who engages in sexual intercourse without love really give his total self? Obviously, *no*. The gift of total self, which the act expresses, is an intense form of commitment. It is the acting out of a full dedication which must be present in fact as well as expression. Otherwise, we destroy the integrity of the act by a lie.

Since commitment must be present for the act of intercourse to be really what it claims, love is an absolute necessity. For love *is* commitment. The terms can be used interchangeably. The individual who engages in premarital sex without love is not committed to his partner. His action speaks clearly: "I have a drive, a need that requires satisfying. I choose you to fulfill it. I have no commitment, no real dedication to you. My action says I am fully dedicated, but I am really not. It doesn't bother me, though. My drive is really the important thing. You exist here to fulfill it. I am using you for my own

The Meaning of the Sex Act

self-gratification."

The result:

> In *The Secular City*, Harvey Cox shows how today's playboy mentality, stressing sex without love, is increasing the feeling and the fact of alienation. When sex excludes love, both partners stay spiritually separated though physically united. The aim of each party is a fleeting moment of mutual self-gratification. The affair is always casual; there is always a conscious avoidance of involvement. The "playmate" becomes a "plaything," a mere accessory, detachable, disposable like Kleenex. This is the stuff of which alienation is made.
> —Mark Link, S.J., *Man in the Modern World* (Chicago, Loyola University Press, 1967), p. 5.

An interesting appendage to the view of love as "commitment" can be made here. The reader may not agree with the following in all its dimensions, but the points seem at least worthy of quite serious reflection.

We have stated that inherent in the act of sexual union is a total gift of self. This would include the idea of commitment to a very intense degree. We cannot really totally give ourselves without it. Expressing such a gift without the deliberate concomitant commitment would be evidence of falsehood. If I am genuine, I cannot express myself so totally, as I do in sexual intercourse, without an exclusive and total dedication as well. Such a dedication has been traditionally termed "marriage."

A priest friend used to drive home this fact to his students with the statement: "If you have sexual intercourse with someone, you are *married* to that individual." The two persons involved may not have gone through the actual marriage ceremony, but honestly, what *is* marriage essentially? As some of our college students are insisting by their marital unions devoid of actual wedding ceremonies, marriage is a total dedication of two persons to each other. The Church has always taught that a marriage can occur without the normally prescribed witnesses (the priest is also a witness) in certain types of situations. Hence the essentials of marriage are carried out by the covenanting parties in their exchange of promises.

If persons object to the statement that they are "married" because of their sexual exchange, the reason they sometimes give is that they had no intention of being married! Our problem is brought thus into clearer focus: Why perform an action that, for all

The Meaning of the Sex Act

practical purposes, says you are married (total self-gift, commitment), if the intention is not to *be* married? Why act out a falsehood?

The individual who continues a sex-for-self-gratification (without love) approach is faced with the problem of growth. He has to ask himself: "As I grow into adulthood, am I going to let mere physical maturity be the sole development taking place? Shouldn't I be doing something to grow in other areas as well—such as the emotional, the psychological?" It is unfortunate perhaps that other areas of growth are not identical to the physical. Body growth is natural. All I normally have to do is cater to hunger and exercise my appetite, and nature takes its course. But other developments are not quite so automatic. I have to sweat to mature in these. If I allow a "come what may" attitude I will probably wind up with a mature body but an immature and ineffective thought life. The world is full of such characters. Do I mind if I someday help swell their ranks?

The most natural thing in life is to be self-centered. A baby clearly shows this. Its world can be adequately described by a circle with arrows around its surface, their points toward the nursery. Contrary to popular belief, the baby's first love is not its mother—but itself. Mom happens to be the person most readily available to fulfill its wants. If the baby is hungry, Mom feeds it. If it is hurt and cries, Mom responds to heal and soothe. If it wants cuddling, Mom usually cuddles it more satisfactorily than anyone else. Everything and everyone exists for the sake of the baby's satisfaction and pleasure. The one-child family can readily give rise to spoiled children as a result. This center-of-attention attitude may continue through the developing years if there is no challenge to it. There is no easier way to describe a spoiled child than "self-centered." Maturity is obviously, then, conditioned by an opposite phenomenon: "other-centeredness."

An opportunity for developing this "other-centeredness" may present itself quite early in a child's life. An example I witnessed readily demonstrates this. My sister had her first child during the first year of marriage—a little girl, Beth. Quite faithful to the normal pattern, Beth readily became the center of existence. She obviously had a utopian life her initial year. But the situation changed not long afterwards.

One day Mommy, who had been away a few days, came home with something like a package in her arms. But this was unlike the usual bundle of groceries with which Beth

The Meaning of the Sex Act

was familiar. Mommy held this one extra close . . . and it even seemed to emit sounds! Beth was intrigued. She wouldn't take her eyes off the "package." Mommy sat down, and Beth cautiously drew near. Her face suddenly flushed with infantile anger and jealousy. She reached out for the intruder and *lashed* at it. Suddenly she realized that she was no longer the "center" of all attention. Something was encroaching on her territory. That "something" was a threat which had to be taken care of!

The sequel to the story is that in a short time, that same object of her original wrath was being gently kissed and hugged by Beth. Her parents had obviously been successful in helping Beth to accept the newcomer, not as a challenge to her self-styled inalienable rights, but as a person like herself, with rights like herself, whom she had to learn to respect and with whom she had to share the avidly sought-after affection and attention. Beth had begun to mature and in an area other than the physical. Little Mike had helped her grow.

Sex is like undeveloped child love. It is naturally self-centered. Somehow growth has to bring it about that when I use the sexual act, it must not be a lie—it must *mean* what it actually *says:* It must express a total self-giving. It can do so only if sex has become not merely a means of self-gratification but an expression of deep love. This does not occur naturally. A person who uses sex in a self-centered way for a long period of time is not going to make a sudden drastic change. We all tend to act as we are. If I am too self-centered sexually, the marital act can become nothing more than a vehicle for self-gratification. Is this perhaps one of the reasons why the sexual act is not sufficiently satisfactory for many married couples? If a man accuses a woman of being sexually frigid, could it be because his approach—entirely centered on self—causes her to be emotionally "chilled"?

Therefore, young people should ask themselves some important questions about sex. In doing so they should try to see more than what is merely on the surface. Also they would best do this before they are too far along in a relationship to be sufficiently objective. Sexual intercourse is too important a reality to be approached without seriousness. When we realize the total gift of self it speaks, and the richness and beauty it is capable of expressing, we ought to handle it in the same manner we do other important occurrences in life. We ought to give it a good deal of thought.

3 IS "LOVE" ALL THAT MATTERS?

IS "LOVE" ALL THAT MATTERS? 3

"Love" — The Problem

WE sometimes hear it said that thoughtful young people today see a problem in the sexual situation in which there is mutual exploitation, when there is no feeling of love present . . . just boy using girl, and vice versa. Such youths, we are told, can readily admit the selfishness in such a relationship and, therefore, the basic wrongness involved. This may be true for some. But there is a counterbalancing trend discernible among the young, a kind of "situation ethics" approach to morality. Many youths are not aware what the words mean, but they tend for all practical purposes to profess some characteristics of that type of morality quite strongly. One of my students wrote: "Premarital sex is a controversial subject today. Is it right or wrong? No one really has the authority to declare it right or wrong . . ." Some students will speak of "each person doing his own thing"; others will add: "If we're in love, why not?"; "It's OK if nobody gets hurt."

There are young people who can see, more or less clearly, a situation of selfish sex in someone they know. Yet they will still take the position: "If they think it's OK, what's wrong with it?" This seems an obvious outgrowth of a moral philosophy devoid of

Is "Love" All That Matters? 35

specific principles of ethical behavior beyond the basic idea of *love*. If there are no directives to guide me in my relationship with people other than: "Do what is the most loving thing," I am left hanging with the problem of discerning what *is* the loving thing in a given situation. As a result of the confused notions of love which many people have today—both young *and* old— there naturally develops a wide range of different actions in these personal relationships which produce many *hurts*. And since just about any action can be considered right if a confused notion of love is in command, "What right do I have to decide something is wrong if someone else thinks otherwise?" The resultant hands-off approach is wholly understandable.

If love is the sole guide with which I confront a situation, that is, if I try to do what I perceive to be the "most loving thing," without really considering other principles or directives, is there not a danger that I actually may not do the most loving thing, despite my good intentions? Each of us has been hurt, now and then, by persons who had no intention of hurting anyone. We usually feel that if they had known the situation better or had given it more thought, another approach would have been made, and we would have escaped injury.

Considering the normal confusion rampant regarding love, the inability, for example, of so many to discern real love from mere passing infatuation, and the making of love synonymous with feeling, it would appear that if our actions regarding important affairs are to remain responsible and thoughtful, we had better bring something else to the situation than that which we may too readily be referring to as "love."

Young people normally believe wholeheartedly in love. Adults who try to teach about it profess the same belief. Those who try to bring to a personal encounter some principles beyond the idea of love alone will usually explain them as being encompassed in that idea of love. As Father Bernard Haring has stated, love is not a principle without a definitive content:

> The thesis of extreme situationists asserts that there is no prohibitory principle that always binds and that everything except love is relative, changeable, and open to varied interpretations. In the final analysis, this means that love is a sphinx, something that looks at once like a human, a lion, a winged creature—an inscrutable thing without a countenance. It could be at the same time concerned about others

Is "Love" All That Matters? 37

and unselfish and also utilitarian and pragmatic. Or it could fall from the sky as atom bombs on Hiroshima and Nagasaki. In Joseph Fletcher's book *Situation Ethics* there are a dozen mutually exclusive definitions of love.— Bernard Haring, *Morality Is for Persons* (Farrar, Straus and Giroux, 1971), p. 126.

"Love" is difficult to describe, almost impossible to define other than by the ultimate definition of St. John: "God is Love!" Those experiencing genuine love tend to feel this is another of those areas where human language is all too inadequate.

Unfortunately, what we sometimes take for love is merely an illusion. Those caught in the thralls of an infatuation, for example, seldom perceive it as such. For them, the infatuation is love. Yet these same individuals, looking back on the relationship later from a more distant and objective viewpoint, will clearly admit that it was definitely not love. But when caught up in the excitement of the infatuation, they think they are experiencing the genuine thing.

But even when we feel love is present, does this make premarital sex "all right"? Are there any solid guiding principles that will assist me in my responsible reflection? Or, is love the only reality that I can bring to this experience? If so, what would this love then mean? Can we say anything about love —or is it destined to remain enclosed in the indescribable?

LOVE — A CLARIFICATION

Joseph Champlin, in his popular book *Don't You Really Love Me?* attempts to arrive at an idea of genuine love through the use of examples. A person who professes to "love" pizza or the "young unattached thing bouncing around his office," for example, does injustice to the word love. The sentiment is purely self-centered, and, as previously shown, self-centeredness can be a clear sign of immaturity.

Everyone knows love is not immature. It is noble, creative, capable of drawing out an individual beyond himself. His life task is to grow from the undeveloped I-centered experience of love that characterizes him as an infant and growing child to the mature status of love capable of giving total self for the sake of the fulfillment of the loved partner. This is the characteristic of every *true* love: self-giving. In Champlin's other examples, the young engaged man who saves his fiancee from an onrushing car but dies in the attempt, and Damien on Molokai, who contracts leprosy in caring for his flock,

Is "Love" All That Matters?

give their lives to save their beloved. The concentration in both cases is on the beloved, not on self: the former an instantaneous gesture, obviously the product of a long and deep other-dedication; the latter a continuous gesture, with a similar other-centered preparation.

In these two examples Champlin is zeroing-in on the idea of self-giving as basic to love. But there is another concept just as clearly involved, namely, that a gift of honest and real love seldom exists without precedent. It is not so much a beginning of love as it is an expression of an already existing love or, at least, of a quality of life capable of making such an other-oriented expression. Self-centered people do not usually perform such actions. They are left for the mature, for the "*other*-centered."

In the area of both love and sex, the natural tendency is to be *self*-centered. We have discussed this already in a previous chapter. Sex, to be mature, must be an expression of love. Such an intense pleasure will normally always have a good bit of self involved, but the important point is the direction of concentration. The loved one is at the center of the stage. The giver is working the floodlights, so to speak.

But such a situation is not automatic. It has to be developed over a period of time.

It takes time and intense effort to take my field of concentration away from myself. The task is lifelong. But it should be sufficiently along in development that when I marry, my whole life, including its sexual expression, will already be characterized by that "self-forgetfulness."

Although the sexual act has to be seen as an expression of love, it should not be confused with love. There is a distinction between the two. Either can exist without the other. Sexual intercourse can occur with a prostitute as well as a truly loved one. The former situation is hardly characterized by love! And if a couple is unable to separate the sexual expression from what they feel is a love bond existing between them, that love bond should be definitely questioned. For when times demand the sacrificing of that sexual expression, will love be able to stand on its own? In a bond of true love, the relationship can continue despite the sexual absence.

Somehow, individuals should be able to know whether their sexual attraction for one another is an *expression* of their love or whether it is only sexual attraction:

> It is absolutely necessary for two people to prove to each other by their actions (talk is cheap) that their sexual need for

Is "Love" All That Matters?

one another is really subordinate to their love. If a young man says, in effect, "I love you; therefore, I must have you," he is saying very convincingly that he cannot or does not distinguish love from sex. If he cannot demonstrate his love for his fiancee by forgoing its genital expression now, will he ever be able to do so later on in marriage?—O'Neil and Donovan, *Sexuality and Moral Responsibility* (Corpus Books, World Publishing Co., New York, N.Y.), p. 134.

Because of the all-engrossing character of sexual intercourse, it can easily become a giant overshadowing and blocking out everything else in a relationship. As someone has stated so aptly, at a time when young people should be exploring personalities, they often are exploring bodies instead. Sex can become almost a totality, but if it does so, it is usually swift to pass. Without a foundation, it is shallow and like all other realities whose appeal is superficial, its life expectancy is very limited. A marriage for sex can easily result; and when the sex attraction departs, as it will indeed depart in such a situation, nothing is left but the unwanted hurts.

In order to prevent such an unfortunate happening, a relationship must be built between two individuals—a relationship that will express itself in the sexual act so that the latter has a context and a definite meaning. If such a relationship can be properly established, sex will no longer be a self-enclosed entity but one that has a depth of meaning and significance.

A community of love has to be constructed by a man and a woman. We use the term "constructed" because love is not a romantic happening so much as it is the result of much effort.

A feeling for another person may be superficial and passing (infatuation) or the beginnings of a really deep love. But in either case, it is a *beginning,* something that has to be continued in the only way it can continue to any lasting extent: through the building of a foundation that will support the feeling and enable it to be the expression of something other than itself. A feeling expressing only itself can too easily be like the blind leading the blind. The only way we can be assured that it is genuine is by giving it a definite meaning. That meaning can be found in a life of commitment, sacrifice, and other-centeredness which the sexual act can then express. If we begin with the sexual expression too soon, its all-pervasive and obsessive tendency tends to thwart efforts in these other areas. Again, the loving relationship must be *first* established so that intercourse has something to "say."

What have we seen about love so far? It is difficult to define, but its characteristics can be described. It is a feeling, yes, but there is a danger of confusing it with infatuation. However, whether initially an infatuation or not, the feeling can develop into true love if it is accompanied by certain traits. Love must be essentially self-giving and other-centered because true love is mature and normally found only in adults. This is evident because of the normal self-centeredness of the infant and child. Where self is in the middle of the stage, real love is not yet present. That only comes when self becomes a spotlight focused on the other person.

CAN TEENS TRULY LOVE?

Some authors seriously question the ability of teens to actually love. While a dogmatic statement on this point would be highly inappropriate, there still seems to be some truth here. We cannot emphatically state that teenagers are incapable of genuine love, but certain aspects of their development at this stage of maturity seem opposed to what characterizes true love.

Psychology has shown that the main goal

of the adolescent is to find a definite "self." Life is not a static reality. It is dynamic. It is constantly growing, changing, "becoming" in accord with its innate potentials and the environmental factors conditioning and affecting such potentials. Man is an evolving being. From his youngest years he begins to reach out and touch, experiment, discover. He soon learns that there is a someone who is doing that searching and grasping and he spends his growing years trying to clearly perceive that someone.

During the teen years he applies his developing mind to the vast physical and emotional changes he is experiencing. Even in the ideal situation where the physical and psychic develop evenly, he is still not sure enough of the "self" going through all the changes. There has not been enough reflection to produce the requisite insights for such a clear "self" view.

But how many situations *are* ideal? Many persons do not develop evenly on all levels. For some, physical development is ahead of the intellectual. For others, the field is reversed, and the intellectual takes precedence. How often is the emotional waylaid in this growth process and only quite belatedly woven into the human fabric?

With the new insights he acquires as the

Is "Love" All That Matters?

maturity process unfolds and is developed, the adolescent finds the "I" too new in all its changes. It doesn't allow him a clear concept. What is that "I"? Where is it going? What are its true characteristics? As time goes by, he will understand it more clearly especially through his peer and adult relationships. But as yet, the self is quite hazy.

All of this causes a problem with love. If love is essentially a gift of self, it must presuppose a knowledge of the self given. If I give myself completely to another, I must know relatively clearly who I am. Before I give myself, I have to find myself. And although that search is admittedly a lifelong process, it requires a certain degree of discovery before it can be adequately given.

A too-early gift produces a later retraction. There is too much change in adolescence to permit a sufficiently stabilized offering. Those who attempt it through a teenage marriage often find themselves too much changed in just a few years after the ceremony. The partner who seemed complete fulfillment only two years earlier now seems vastly different. For who can predict how evenly two developments will proceed? There is no guarantee of a parallel development in the young. And while love can effect a great deal in drawing two people together and easing problems that present themselves in a mature relationship, it should not be expected to perform miracles if the individuals involved are not sufficiently developed. The ideal is to wait until the boy and girl are far enough along in their growth to possess rather stable selves. A definite age can hardly be set for such a development since each individual possesses his own unique growth characteristics. But it should be obvious that the younger the person is, the greater the chance of such a relatively stable self being absent.

* * *

Sex, a beautiful expression of love, must be clearly understood as something that can be considered apart from love. Otherwise, individuals may confuse it with love. They may be viewing it as the substance of their love rather than as its expression. To prevent this from occurring, sex should not be entered into until the relationship is developed and established on other levels. This takes time. And since love grows with time and effort, whereas infatuation is sudden and passing, the feeling that continues to pervade the relationship and deepen through it will be all the more clearly seen as the genuine thing.

Love focuses on the beloved rather than

Is "Love" All That Matters?

on self. Furthermore, it is long lasting. It allows the other to grow in the way he desires without craving immediate responses. It allows the individuals involved to work and live more joyful and productive lives rather than inhibit activity as does mere infatuation. It can *wait!* And it does not grow cold in waiting. It can enable one to see much in the beloved that escapes the vision of others, but at the same time it is not blinded to deficiencies. It readily admits them and perceives how it can overcome them, or at least help to overcome them. It is truthful, an essential trait of any honest relationship. Trust is another reality that does not exist in a vacuum. Trust must be prepared for. An individual cannot be expected to trust another if the latter has done little to support such trust. Love should be able to forgive fully and to try just as fully to forget. But actions of the other partner should support such a gesture and make it reasonable.

"If I am in love, that is all that is necessary" can now be better understood. Yes, love is sufficient if we grasp what love means. I bring to a situation more than a general abstract word, a simple feeling. I bring a developed relationship that the sexual act then expresses. This presupposes an extended period of time in which such a relationship has been worked out and will continue to be worked out.

Our next point is perhaps more difficult to handle: "Why wait till marriage if true love is now already present?" We shall treat this in the following chapters.

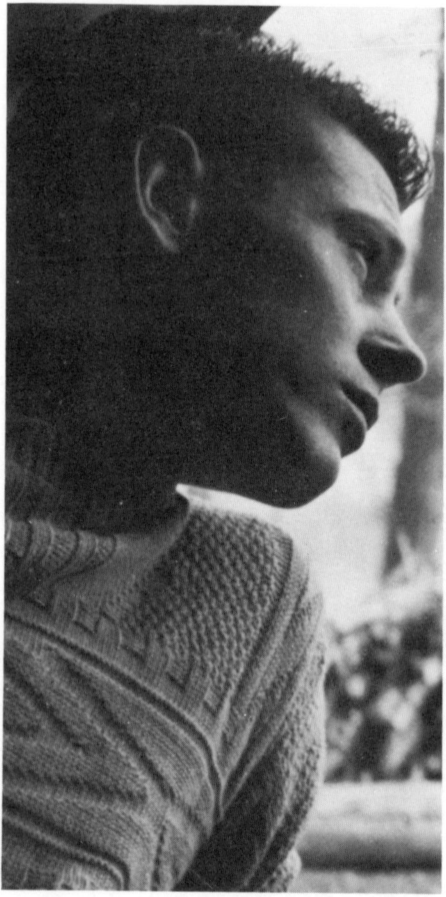

4 WHY WAIT TIL MARRIAGE?

STUDENTS often express displeasure concerning "one-sided" treatments of premarital sex: that is, they disapprove when only the "why nots" are discussed; whereas, to their mind, the reasons for going ahead are completely ignored.

In all honesty, I have difficulty dealing with the reasons in favor of premarital sex. That there are some plausible arguments is obvious; otherwise, the thoughtful young people sincerely asking the question: "If we really love each other, why wait till marriage?" would not be doing so. But I do have my own honest, sincere beliefs. I have heard many of the reasons of students who differ with me, but I cannot find them totally convincing. Too many red lights keep flashing—not orange, which would signal to proceed with caution. My lights indicate a total stop! And I cannot get the car moving again because of all the traffic obstacles, the chief of which are "wisdom of the past" and "insights of the present" from both young and old.

I could take out time to cite (and sort of acquiesce in) the reasons I have heard in favor of premarital sex. But what would this accomplish? I would be doing so only for the sake of making an impression. To me that would be literary prostitution. I can only present the approach I truly see and

Why Wait Till Marriage?

trust that others will respect it in the spirit in which it is offered.

You have all, at some time or other, come across reasons in favor of waiting for full sexual expression until marriage. Some of these reasons you may be disregarding completely because, as you see it, they are obviously irrelevant. Others you may accept fully; some perhaps, only partially. I would like to deal, in this chapter, with what I consider to be some of the more convincing reasons against premarital sex.

Besides the ideas presented in previous chapters we could add the following:

1. An unwanted child is still a possibility, since no contraceptive to date is totally safe other than complete continence.*

2. Guilt feelings can play a real part in the affair. We cannot dismiss, as easily as we may sometimes believe, values and morals we have learned in the past.

3. Despite the feelings of many that they would not mind a non-virgin for a mate, or perhaps even desire one, many young people still see a tremendous value in the person who has saved this ultimate sexual expression for that really special

---

*Cf. Edward Stevens, S.J., *Making Moral Decisions* (Paulist Press, New York, 1969), pp. 108-109. Stevens indicates "the pregnancy rate in terms of number of children per hundred women per year" for the various contraceptives.

individual who will be a life companion. This person as that "life companion" is not fully assured until the actual public ceremony takes place.

4. Instead of looking upon the honeymoon as a possible clumsy blunder if sex is something completely new, there seems to be a more beautiful view of the honeymoon, that is, as a time of joy in sharing with the partner that initial experience with its possible deficiencies, and of growing together from the very beginning toward that rich sexual fulfillment that is only realized gradually over a period of years in marriage.

5. Fidelity is a tremendous value in any marriage, and anything that may undermine the trust that must exist between partners should be avoided at all costs. Premarital sex may cause one of the partners to wonder if he or she was the first of the other's sexual partners. Then arises the fearful question that if there were another or others, how will the partner act after marriage? Even if this were the first such sexual experience, the fear may still remain that . . .

> If two people can rationalize sexual intercourse with one another before marriage, against the commonly accepted code of most religions and civil society on the grounds that they "love

Why Wait Till Marriage?

each other," no vows pronounced before a minister or magistrate in ten minutes are going to eliminate similar rationalizations for adultery after marriage.—O'Neil and Donovan, *op. cit.,* pp. 136-137.

There seem to be ample statistical studies backing up the fact that those who play before marriage find it easier to stray after marriage. Those who enter marriage as virgins find adultery a very hard step indeed.

6. A recent Northwestern University study* showed a real difference in what was termed the "frequency of request" rate for sexual intercourse. Men tended to ask for intercourse much more frequently if they had no intention of marrying the girl, and much less frequently if the intention was more strongly present. This demonstrates the different value men tend to place upon the special girl of their choice. The potential marriage partners hold important places in their esteem, and their behavior clearly reflects it.

Dr. Gebhard, a fellow worker with the famous Dr. Kinsey, did a recent national

---

*Information cited here is taken from the records of Dr. and Mrs. J. C. Willke, *Sex . . . Should We Wait?* (Hiltz Publ. Co., 1969), a live recording of a talk to 500 students at the University of Cincinnati.

sampling and found information to substantiate the Northwestern study. A majority of college women (50-60 percent) had their first intercourse because they loved the man involved and intended to marry him. An additional 20-25 percent loved the man and "hoped" to marry him. Briefly then, around 75-80 percent of college women who give themselves totally to a man are in love with him and plan to, or hope to marry him.

Men showed an enormous difference here. Only about 12 percent planned to marry the girl! Another 20-25 percent had, as they put it, "some emotional attachment" to the girl but had no intent to marry.

This is a rather striking comparison, and it tends to clarify the way a man and woman look at initial partners. It should also show support for the often-stated fact that men tend to be freer with a girl they are not seriously considering as their future marriage partner. The latter has to be different!

7. Feelings come and go in any relationship. The intent of marriage is to stabilize the union for the good of the couple involved and any offspring they may have. Too much of self is, so to speak, "put on the line" in the total dedication inherent in sexual intercourse. No woman, in

Why Wait Till Marriage? 57

particular, can walk from such a union without leaving a big piece of herself behind. The intention is, of course, to have the couple sufficiently prepared for the union before it occurs. The obligations that come from the public ceremony tend thus not only to safeguard a commitment once made but also to raise a sign of caution for those who have not yet made that step.

8. It is sometimes stated that letting off sexual steam through intercourse has the wholesome effect of diminishing bothersome strains in the relationship. This objection shows little insight into the process of maturing. We have heard time and again that nothing good comes in life except through hard work. We have failed, however, to apply this to some important areas, including the sexual. The sexual strains and stresses present in the association of a young man and woman are normal and healthy. They are, in fact, *essential* for sexuality to become the mature aspect of life it must be in a full adult. Giving in to those pressures does nothing to foster their proper development. Control of one's sexual drive is essential to adulthood. If a couple cannot manifest such control before marriage, will they be able to do so after marriage when situations arise demanding self-control? Marriage is not a complete sexual heyday;

sex must be both controlled and respectfully utilized if its beauty is to remain a continuing value. Genuine love gives rise to the right kind of purity, which in turn creates even more love. This purity does so both before and after the marriage ceremony.

9. Should not a couple have intercourse before the marriage ceremony in order to test if one is frigid or unable to adjust sexually to the other in proper fashion? Well, if the intent is merely to see if they can physically unite, a simple doctor's examination would do the trick. That is no problem. If the intent is to discover if the couple can relate sexually in the broader emotional aspects, an occasional total gift of self will hardly accomplish the desired results. There are several problems involved.

First, as we briefly indicated above, the sexual adjustment that makes for true and rich fulfillment of both partners is not something that is brought about immediately. The process is one of long duration. We can speak of months, perhaps even several years of intimate lovemaking that will be required for many individuals. Part of the beauty of the process is the mutual search and discovery that each goes through in the relaxed atmosphere of a stable and permanent union. Discovering

Why Wait Till Marriage?

things with the one you love is always a rewarding activity. There is no threat of embarrassment or rejection when the search is mutual.

Furthermore, there is a real possibility that what I discover through a premarital sex experience will be a misunderstood "frigidity." Let us imagine, for example, that Tom is deeply in love with Mary. They have been able to develop a very rewarding relationship and have decided to marry soon. Tom has heard of the "frigid" woman possibility and is anxious to discover if this might be the only serious problem in their otherwise ideal union. He and Mary go "all the way" one night, and Tom's world collapses. His fears are realized. Mary was nonresponsive. Tom tries again later, and finds the same reaction. He is convinced they will never be able to relate properly on this level. They break the engagement. We have two deeply hurt people.

What Tom did not realize was that Mary, who had deep-seated convictions against any premarital experience, was unable to give herself to him properly outside a marriage bond. The "frigidity" Tom experienced in her was nothing more than Mary's subconscious reserve regarding premarital sex. She would have responded the same to any man. She is, actually, not cold at all. On the contrary, if Tom would have waited until marriage, he would have found Mary a warm, receptive, loving marital partner. Their premature and disillusioned breakup was totally unnecessary. Who can measure the irreparable harm done by such an uncalled-for venture?

10. The most difficult objection of all to answer is the one that is irrational. A student expressed it this way: "Father, no matter what, if two people want to do it, they are going to do it." Another added: "Why do you have to have reasons? Why not go by how you feel?" Persons who make such statements are not looking for answers. They are like the child who cries and, when asked why, merely responds: "Because!" There is no logical reason given.

A child frequently does not need reasons to regulate his mode of action. He does things simply "because." However, there is always something behind how we act, whether it is on a conscious or unconscious level. We do things for reasons. We scratch our face because it itches. We eat because we are hungry. We sleep because we are tired. It is a sign of a mature adult to be able to recognize what lies behind the more important actions he performs. He is accountable for how he behaves; he must

Why Wait Till Marriage?

be responsible for his actions.

Therefore, to engage in premarital sex simply because "I want to" is to forfeit maturity and to bring instead to the situation a juvenile frame of mind. If these persons can be brought to understand the immaturity involved in such an objection, and instead to realize that there are ramifications growing out of their behavior that go beyond the simple act viewed in itself, then perhaps they will be more hesitant to proceed on simple "feeling" or "want" alone.

* * *

A book such as Evelyn Millis Duvall's *Why Wait Till Marriage?* contains numerous other reasons for premarital chastity. Our intent in this chapter was to include some reflections on questions posed by adolescents who found other sources wanting or perhaps insufficient. The reader is encouraged to peruse the popular work of Duvall for a much broader discussion of the problem. It will help to fill in what is lacking above and assist the reader to survey most of the traditional reasons for control. Many of these traditional reasons are still solidly valid.

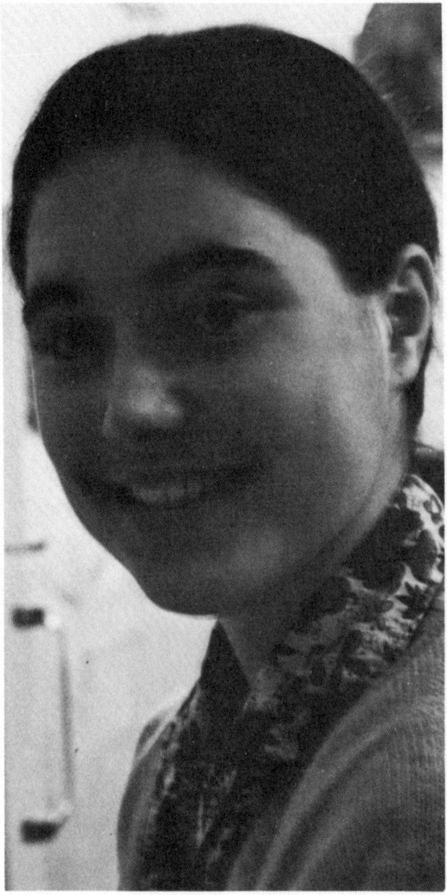

WHAT DOES GOD WANT? 5

OUR discussions so far have dealt almost exclusively with levels other than the specifically religious. This has not been done on the supposition that religion has nothing to offer. That would indeed be a misconception. What we have been trying to show is that religious principles and beliefs have a definite foundation. They are not restrictions dreamed up by individuals isolated from real life. They are not formulated just to oppose me but are intimately involved *in* me. They are meant for my own good and actually place a crown on values I am able to believe in on a purely human level.

An interesting phenomenon today is the discovery of the unifying agreement of psychology, human experience, and true Christian morals. Christ's command of love, given to his followers for all time, finds psychology and human experience in total agreement. Psychologists regard such love as best for man, for his own continuing good.

The developing field of psychology substantiates the importance of love as stressed by Christianity's founder. Love is seen by both as a needed bond between men in order to allow them to live at peace and in harmony with themselves and others. Love causes man to mature, to grow, to realize his many potentials. It also causes the

What Does God Want?

recipient of his love to be fulfilled, and thus to grow.

Man's past experience adds its own agreement to love's value. When people live in the union that only love can bestow, the problems that confront their lives have a solid basis for proper resolution. A clear example is the effect friendship (a form of love) can have between heads of state. The deeper and more sincere the relationship, the greater the cordiality and the fewer the hostilities between countries. This may seem a simplistic political analysis, but the element of truth is there. We cannot unequivocally label all relationships between heads of state as merely feigned for the sake of political gain.

One function of religious moral principles is to reinforce and more emphatically state the important directives for man's good that science and experience offer. Moral principles are thus binding because they are there to protect man. They protect him not only in his relationship with other men but also from himself. No man has a right to hurt even himself.

Moral directives forbid certain actions which tend to harm self or others. They guard man's relations with his fellowmen so that all can grow in the bonds of love and unity that man's social nature requires. And they guard man's relations with God so that man will grow in his image and in the love that God wills to be the bond between himself and his creatures.

Religious principles reflect God's will for man as man has come, through prayer, experience and reflection, to discover that will. In an important sense God's will is somewhat different for all men: Each has his own special calling or vocation. But fundamental to the varieties of God's call is his general will which is present to all men: to grow in love for one another and in love for God. What this means has been in many instances discovered by man—often through serious mistakes.

One solid rule that has resulted from mature Christian reflection over the ages is quite precise: No fornication! This realization is not merely the continuance of some ancient tradition lost in the haze of antiquity. It is a directive that has found continual support through the years as an outgrowth of that primary love command. Reasons, such as the ones listed above and earlier in this book, provide the other-than-religious basis. But religion itself provides an added thrust in the direction of continence.

St. Paul, one of the leading figures of the early Church, speaks about marriage as a mystery. His teaching can be found in the

What Does God Want?

fifth chapter of his letter to the Ephesians. The marital union symbolizes and reflects the love Christ has for his Church. It is also a sign of the covenant formed between Yahweh and the Jewish people in the Old Testament. As the husband and wife discover the tremendous joys that their love-union produces in their lives, they can more clearly perceive how God loves us, his chosen people, today.

What is marriage? Essentially it is two things: the solemn promise man and woman make to live and love together, and the actual living of that promise. But we cannot view marriage as merely a private affair between two persons. It goes beyond them to the social community of which they form a part. It would be more correct to say that marriage is not only a promise to live and love together, but to love beyond themselves—to share with others the beauty of love. Marriage not only consists of a promise between the persons forming the loving covenant-bond, but comprises as well a statement to the community that an adventure has begun for its good as well. The love husband and wife express is not meant to be turned in solely upon themselves, but to extend beyond. Such a broader extension must be present if there is true love, for love is expanding, not restricting. It must go out to others to be able to bloom.

A beautiful way to express this social dimension of marriage can be done within the ceremony. The couple could turn to the assembled relatives and friends, who symbolize and represent the entire community, and recite their vows to them as well as to themselves.

Since Christ acts through his sacraments, Christ acts through marriage. And since essential to marriage is the living of the love promise, every action of the married state is a source of grace. That includes the sexual act.

But the sexual act is different from other actions of a married couple's lives. Through it the spouses not only express and foster mutual love, but also co-create with God a new member of the human community. This is a very sacred function. While admittedly the act need not always be performed by them with the intention of propagation, such propagation is essentially bound up with the sexual expression. Why? Because that is the way it is done! No amount of kissing or rubbing of noses will bring about an additional human being! I may separate in my mind the functions of reproduction and lovemaking, but sexual intercourse in itself speaks no such division. Both are part and parcel of this intense

What Does God Want?

self-offering.

There is thus a very special place in the economy of marriage for the total gift of love. It has been given by God a significance and sacredness all its own. To perform the sexual act outside the marriage bond is to attempt to remove from the act Christ in his sacramental presence. It is an attempt to snatch it from its God-intended matrimonial environment, with all the blessings that God bestows upon it, and to construct instead a self-determined context for its use. Whether realized by the partners or not, this approach pits the individuals against God. There is implied the idea that God does not always know best. The "sacramental" act that brings Christ's love to the couple and intensifies their solemnly promised union in the marriage vows now finds itself robbed of this spiritual dimension and in danger instead of causing division between the participants. Premarital sex is thus a misuse, an irreverence, quite simply, a *wrong*.

* * *

The public "I do" proclamation thus offers a wealth of significance once we are able to penetrate the simple surface. Here is another example of what we discussed in our first chapter: a value delicately shielded from superficial observance.

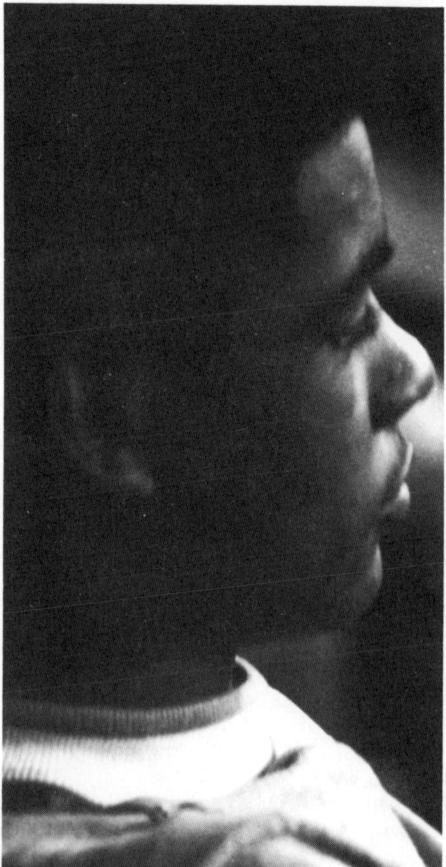

A DIRECTION TO FOLLOW 69

WHEN discussing premarital sex with my students I have always tried to allow an atmosphere of free discussion. Pros and cons usually fill the air so fully that when the time is over, some students complain that everything was left "hanging." They ask me to be clear in my stand so that they can understand my position as well as that of fellow students.

I have tried to be clear in previous chapters on views I hold and believe in very much. I would like to continue to be so in this chapter, while explaining in a little more detail the way I feel young people should act in order to protect the many areas premarital sex could affect.

There are aspects of the situation ethics controversy that I can appreciate and accept. Men are not made for laws, but laws for men. No law can be absolute if to apply it here and now would be a contradiction to real love.

I cannot, however, envisage *any* situation where premarital sex would be a *clear* indication of true love. Many times the act may indeed seem to be such an expression, but we are again faced with a situation whose real context is much broader and deeper than first appears on the surface. Such a situation is like an iceberg: There is much more below the surface that has to be

A Direction to Follow

taken into account if we are to grasp the total reality.

When a man and woman are in love and are moved to express this love in the total gift of self, they are inspired by what is the "most loving thing to do" here and now. Under the influence of passion they can hardly be expected to launch into a whole set of mental gymnastics. When emotions are intensely involved, the mind has difficulty holding what, at other more objective times, is its normal sway. It is better, therefore, to consider the problem before the heart and passions take control.

What is the situation in which they find themselves when the desire to express their union bodily arises? It is not merely boy and girl alone in a car parked on an untraveled road during a warm summer evening with a soft breeze and bright moon adding to the pleasant atmosphere. That is all that meets the casual eye. However, the context of this situation is much broader. All the red lights of previous chapters start to flash on. These also comprise this given situation. There are many signals pointing out that the *best* thing *(the most loving thing!)* to do would not be what they are perhaps so ardently pulled toward doing. These signals are so strong that the couple could hardly proceed with assurance that what they are about to undertake is "so right." The most loving thing to do would be to play it safe rather than to chance a hurt to the one who is loved so much. Nothing should be done to rob the relationship of its beauty and nobility.

We are not stating here that the sexual act is something ugly. It remains a beautiful expression of love whether before or after marriage if it is between two people in love seeking to express love. The wrong involved is due to its untimeliness, its lack of sufficient safeguards to protect its value, and its potential explosive nature in an improperly prepared and not sufficiently secure setting.

In our discussion so far of premarital sex, we have seemingly been directly concerned with the total expression alone. This can be rather misleading, however. The impression may be that there is a neat division between acts of lovemaking preliminary to the total gift and the concrete act of full sexual intercourse. Nothing could be farther from the truth. Indeed, some students clearly see a connection: "If kissing and other acts of lovemaking are all right, why is sexual intercourse not permitted?"

To envisage sexual intercourse as separate from heavy petting and passionate kissing is to create a dichotomy where none

A Direction to Follow

really exists. The act of human copulation is distinguished in *degree alone* from its preliminaries. Together they comprise what we can term a "continuum," a unified entity that begins when the first sexual stimulations are experienced. Once the process is set in motion, once the sexual drive is "ignited," its logical culmination is intercourse.

It is because of this connection between the initial sexual stirrings and their ultimate fulfillment that problems can arise when individuals attempt a "turning off" once the "turning on" has begun. There is a frustration experienced that becomes increasingly stronger to the degree that the stimulation has progressed. If such a behavior has been sufficiently prolonged, it can actually produce impotency in the person concerned. His pattern of sexual response has been so consistently one of beginning but never finishing that a deeply entrenched habit has resulted. When the time comes for him to carry the drive through to its conclusion, he finds himself "blocked."

Furthermore, such a clear distinction between the full act and what precedes it would be catering to an obnoxious legalistic mode of action. If intercourse alone is the forbidden fruit, any mode of behavior would be justified so long as there is no physical penetration. The "legal virgin" whose hymen is intact becomes queen par excellence despite her bodily availability to every passionate playboy in town. The advocates of such a mechanical definition of virginity would find their students using similar mental gymnastics to rationalize any behavior short of complete physical union. Such an approach would not be that of a true Christian moralist.

The solution to the problems involved in stopping short after sexual preliminaries is not to go in the exact opposite direction: a full act in each instance! Besides the difficulties we have discussed previously, there is the added problem of "a point of no return." Once a couple have gone all the way, they usually find it hard to limit their lovemaking to a lesser level which will offer little, or no, satisfaction. Unless they are in a covenant-bond of marriage that allows freedom and a relaxed atmosphere to continue to the full gift of self, such lovemaking produces the emotional and psychological dissatisfactions that are not to the couple's best interests. It would be far better not to set in motion the powerful sex drives in the first place.

This does not mean that an engaged couple should act like robots. Their relationship must be one of warmth and depth. But

A Direction to Follow

each should recognize sufficiently how the other reacts to and is affected by certain manifestations of love. As their association becomes more frequent and of longer duration, there naturally develops a strong tendency for fuller physical union. Realizing that they cannot afford to allow themselves to go all the way at this time, they should regulate carefully their loving companionship so as to prevent occurrences conducive to the full act.

We can be sure this is not easy. There will be times when they find it exceedingly difficult to hold off. But the control they show on such occasions will prove the depth of their convictions and the ability they will have to manifest similar self-sacrifice in later married life situations. The less they do directly to cause themselves serious arousal, the more easy such self-regulation will prove to be.

However, the restraint necessary for sexual control cannot be exercised on the level of action alone. An act is always an expression of something. It puts into effect that which is already in existence in the mind. We will always have such a case when the action is other than a purely automatic stimulus-response. This fact can be expressed more succinctly: as a person thinks, so he acts.

Control, then, is necessary not only physically but also *mentally*. If thoughts of a sexual nature are allowed rampant freedom in the mind, it is only a matter of time before they find concrete expression. If there is need to regulate a pattern of sexual behavior in one's relationship with a person of the opposite sex, there must be self-control in the realm of thoughts as well.

Prayer has an important part to play in all this. We believe in a God who not only created us but loves and continues to help and guide us in our lives. We feel that opening ourselves to him and asking for his assistance is not a reach into nothingness but is putting our hand into his and walking with him in our daily adventures. Such divine direction, when sincerely requested and faithfully followed, can do marvels in helping us to control our sexual drives.

* * *

It is an interesting observation that in a time such as ours when the word "freedom" is suffering the same misunderstanding as the word "love," any position that seems restrictive is easily labeled "archaic" or "obsolete." All restrictions are "prudery." Many people do not want regulations of any kind. They confuse freedom with anarchy. And in doing so they fail to recognize that when anarchy is the prevailing condition in

A Direction to Follow

any area, no such thing as freedom is possible. For freedom demands protection for its exercise, and such protection exists in the form of laws, regulations, direction. I am free to *do* if I am first free to be *able* to do!

The position of this chapter is a restrictive one, but it is not anti-free. In fact, it is solidly *pro-free*. The restrictions exist for the sake of genuine freedom of sexual expression: to allow sex to be and to do what it has the potential to do if performed in the proper context.

But sex can be free to express all its deep, warm, and lasting meaning only if its use is adequately restricted. An unprepared or not sufficiently protected adventure can destroy much of the beauty possible in the act. It can take away an important part of the meaning the sexual act can express in the marital union. Any suggested approach that guards that value can hardly be labeled a foe of freedom.

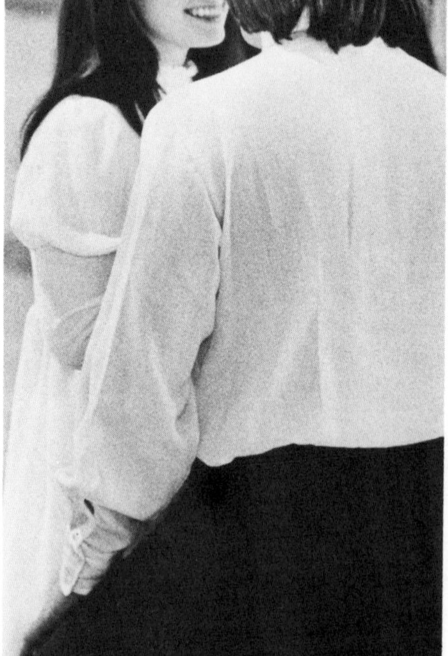

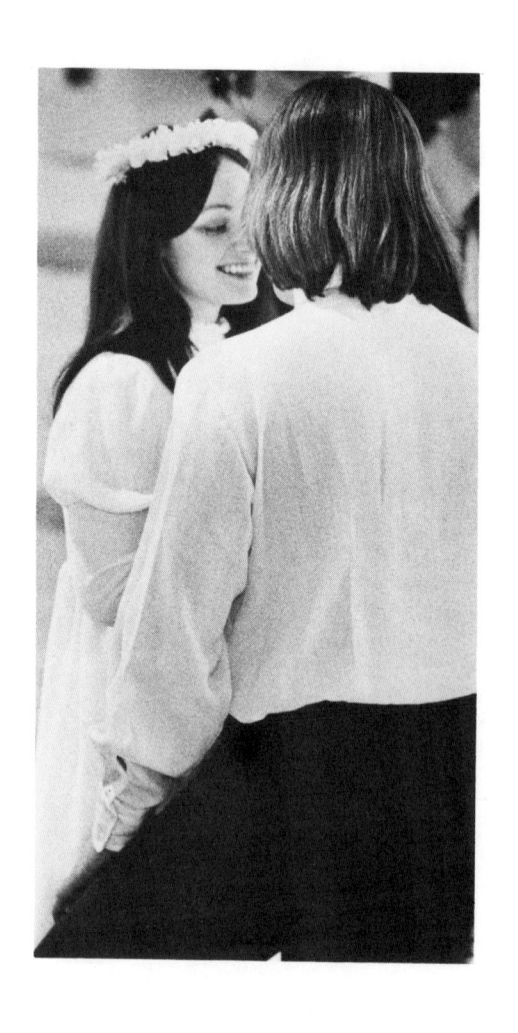

7 I LOVE YOU FOREVER!

7 I LOVE YOU FOREVER!

DR. Clifford Rose Adams, a Pennsylvania researcher-psychologist, has made a lengthy 30-year study of approximately 6,000 couples.* His findings are informative and, frankly, frightening. Because of disparity in male and female sexual interest, Dr. Adams feels that 75 percent of American marriages are a failure!

"When a couple gaze into each other's eyes with what they think is love and devotion, they are not seeing the same thing," he states. The male ranks sex as the second most important factor in a marriage; whereas, his female partner puts it in sixth place. The man subconsciously considers companionship as the only important factor that takes precedence over sex. The female, conversely, seeks love-affection-sentiment, security, companionship, home and family and community acceptance—all before sex.

With such a divergence of desires, we can imagine the problems marriages can have. According to Dr. Adams, marriages do have problems and to an extent one would hardly imagine. Government statistics show that 28 percent of all marriages end in divorce. This figure is misleading, however,

---

*"When you say 'I do' the odds say you won't," an article in the *New York Sunday News,* July 13, 1969. Adams presented his findings to the Identity Research Institute in Washington, D.C.

I Love You Forever!

because it does not include annulments and desertions, which together bring the broken marriage total to almost 40 percent. If we then add "morbidity" marriages, where the couples continue to live under the same roof for appearance or convenience while actually hating each other, we are left with the surprisingly *un*happy figure of only 25 percent as really happy marriages. "The other 75 percent are a bust."

Many of these disasters are caused by "body heat," says Dr. Adams. That is, sexual compatibility is the foundation for such marriages.

It is not surprising then that we have such a disaster. Marriage is more than sex, whether sex is the only value or too important a value in the midst of several others. Sex becomes disproportionate in such a bond. It tries to stand on its own two feet, but it cannot! Sex has, as previously stated, no meaning outside that which it is expressing. A context is necessary, a relationship that incorporates the sexual expression as a sign of deep values. When sex is used without such a foundation, its appeal cannot last. If it has nothing to "say" other than itself, it soon becomes dumb.

Dr. Adams's study uses statistics, and these present a problem for some individuals. "I am not a statistic," I have heard adolescents object. "When I hear such categorizing, I'm just turned right off!"

True, individuals are not statistics, in an important sense. But individuals make up such figures. *That* is fact! They wouldn't exist without people. It is true that we cannot neatly stack men and women in prearranged slots, we must respect their uniqueness and differences. But if certain patterns of behavior tend to produce, as experience shows, certain kinds of results, we would be wise to consider seriously the results no matter how disturbing they might be.

Certain high-cholesterol foods should not be consumed in large amounts if we want to prevent possible heart trouble. Chronic inactivity "revenged" by imprudent overexercise can produce physical ailments in many people. Food with a high concentration of mercury can be disastrous. We hear such warnings daily, and the wise man heeds them. They are all based on facts, figures, "statistics," if you like. They are meant as warning signals to *help* people to live more healthy and lengthy lives. They are not sadistic directives of unbalanced doctors and researchers.

Statistics have been found in several places in this book. They manifest important tendencies. We would like to help young

I Love You Forever!

people to prepare for a life of fulfillment and happiness, and we have used such figures to guide them in their planning. Our intent has not been to categorize people impersonally, but to develop them very personally. Development is self-directed, but it also must necessarily be influenced by information from outside.

Your marriage will be unique; no other will be exactly like it. Yet you will be entering marriage with the hopes and expectations that others before you have also shared together. Many of these individuals have found their dreams destroyed after sometimes only a few years together. What caused the breakups? Were they sudden and unperceived? Or were they the ultimate culmination of some long process of gradual alienation?

In all probability, the causes were of long duration. False concepts of love, "love" without solid foundations, lack of communication, misconceptions in male-female psychology, a love perhaps really present but too often taken for granted—some of these reasons, perhaps only one, perhaps all, could be at the root of each marital failure.

The point is: *You are different.* You can prevent catastrophe in your own marriage. But you will be able to do so only if you *clearly recognize* that you are *not* so very different in another sense. The same causes of marital failure in others will be *your* downfall if you do not recognize that such problems can affect you as well. You will *be* different if you learn from the hard experiences of others. You will be different if the love that is genuinely yours at the time of the ceremony will not be taken for granted, but worked on and shielded from the all too many pitfalls that seem to prey upon young couples today.

Attitudes toward premarital sex have an extremely important part to play in future marriage success. To recognize this is to face reality. To ignore it is to court disaster. Others besides you have faced the problem. Not all have, unfortunately, chosen wisely. It is the author's hope and prayer that your decision will be one of chastity—will be one of waiting until the love that you so ardently desire to express can adequately say what it cries out to say: "I love you. I wish *nothing* but the best for you. I intend to make of our union a lasting expression of the tenderness and deep dedication that we feel for each other now, and to grow to those heights of love that every poet of every age has so painstakingly, yet somehow always inadequately, tried to express in the words so simply phrased: 'I love you forever.'"